Celebrating Hindu FESTIVALS

LIZ MILES

raintree
a Capstone company — publishers for children

Raintree is an imprint of Capstone Global Library Limited, a company incorporated in England and Wales having its registered office at 7 Pilgrim Street, London, EC4V 6LB – Registered company number: 6695582

www.raintree.co.uk
myorders@raintree.co.uk

Edited by James Benefield
Designed by Steve Mead
Original illustrations © Capstone Global Library Limited 2015
Picture research by Eric Gohl
Production by Helen McCreath
Originated by Capstone Global Library Limited
Printed and bound in China

ISBN 978 1 406 29768 3
19 18 17 16 15
10 9 8 7 6 5 4 3 2 1

British Library Cataloguing in Publication Data
A full catalogue record for this book is available from the British Library.

Acknowledgements
Alamy: Homer W Sykes, 29, ImageDB, 24, Marco Secchi, 23, Nisarg Lakhmani, 14, Philippe Hays, 25, Piero Cruciatti, 7, Richard Levine, 17, Werli Francois, 26; Capstone Studio: Karon Dubke, 12–13 (all), 18–19 (all), 34–35 (all); Corbis: Gideon Mendel, 38; Dreamstime: Kadirlookatme, 43 (bottom right); Getty Images: AFP/Prakash Mathema, 42 (bottom), Hindustan Times, 28, IndiaPictures, 42 (top), Jewel Samad, 27, Lonely Planet Images, 10, Stringer, 30, Stringer/AFP, 22, Stringer/Suhaimi Abdullah, 15; iStockphoto: ajijchan, 16, Mlenny, cover, pong6400, 33 (bottom); Newscom: Hindustan Times, 8, 11, 39, Mirrorpix/Richard Swingler, 33 (top), ZUMA Press/Ben Cawthra, 43 (bottom left), ZUMA Press/Monirul Alam, 43 (top), ZUMA Press/Subhash Sharma, 4; Shutterstock: f9photos, 41, Hong Vo, 44, infocus, 9 (right), Kladej, 9 (middle), leoks, 21, Milind Arvind Ketkar, 40, pomxpom, 9 (left), R.M. Nunes, 36, Vladimir Melnik, 37, Wong Yu Liang, 32; SuperStock: age fotostock/Christophe Boisvieux, 31, Robert Harding Picture Library/Godong, 20.

Design Elements: Shutterstock

We would like to thank Peggy Morgan for her invaluable help in the preparation of this book.

SAFETY TIPS FOR THE RECIPES
Trying new recipes is fun, but before you start working in the kitchen, keep these safety tips in mind:
- Always ask an adult for permission, especially when using the hob, oven or sharp knives.
- At the hob, always point saucepan handles away from the edge. Don't keep flammable materials, such as towels, too close to the burners. Have a fire extinguisher nearby. Don't lean too close when you lift a lid off a pan – steam can cause burns, too. Always use oven gloves when taking dishes out of the oven.
- Wash your hands before you work, and wash your workspace and utensils after you are done. Cook foods completely. Don't use expired or spoiled food. Be careful when you cut with knives.
- Work with an adult – together you can both learn about religions of the world through food!

CONTENTS

Introducing Hinduism.................................4

Pongal...8

Holi.. 14

Gods and birthdays.................................20

Diwali...30

Kumbh Mela 36

Family celebrations 38

Celebrations around the world....................42

Find out more..................................... 44

Cookery tips 46

Glossary 47

Index 48

Some words are shown in bold, **like this**. You can find out what they mean by looking in the glossary.

Introducing Hinduism

Hindus believe in an eternal power called Brahman or a personal God who is given various names. Hinduism does not have a **founder** and there is no organization or written beliefs or laws that all Hindus must follow. It is a collection of traditional ways of living, with many Hindus following the same teachings.

>> Crowds of over 100 million people can gather for the Hindu Kumbh Mela pilgrimage. This occurs at a **sacred** river in India.

Around the world

There are between 885 million and 1 billion Hindus, making Hinduism the third largest religion in the world. Although most Hindus live in India, many others live all around the world.

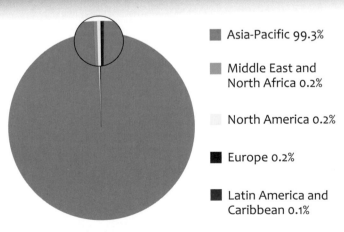

- Asia-Pacific 99.3%
- Middle East and North Africa 0.2%
- North America 0.2%
- Europe 0.2%
- Latin America and Caribbean 0.1%

∧ This chart shows where Hindus can be found in the world.

History

There is no specific event in history that marks the beginning of Hinduism. It formed from many traditions, starting with some practised by the **Indus Valley civilization** around 4,500 years ago. (The name "Hindu" comes from the word "Indus".)

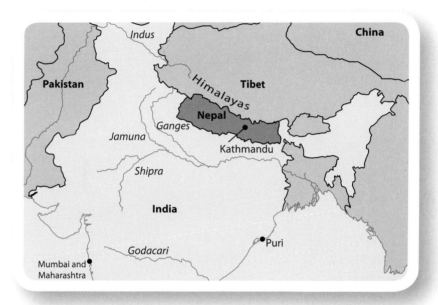

⌃ The Indus Valley, where Hinduism started, is in the north of India and in modern-day Pakistan.

Deities and dharma

- While Hindus say "God is One", they worship **deities** (sometimes called gods). These represent aspects of the One, such as Ganesha, the remover of obstacles.
- **Dharma** is the power that keeps the world and society going. It is believed that every individual has his or her own dharma, too. This dharma is linked to the person's duties and moral values.
- Most Hindus believe that every living thing has an eternal, real self, called atman (sometimes referred to as the spirit or soul).
- It is believed that when a person dies their atman begins a new life in another living "body" (person, animal or plant). This repeated cycle of life is called reincarnation. The law of **karma** means that a person is born into a better or worse life depending on their behaviour in past lives.

Festivals

Some Hindu festivals celebrate the seasons, such as Holi, which marks the beginning of spring. Others celebrate deities, such as Ganesha Chaturthi, which is the birthday of the elephant-headed god, Ganesha.

Food, colours and lights

Hindu festivals include feasting and **fasting**. They are often colourful events and include flowers and light. People throw coloured powders over each other during Holi. Fireworks are set off at Diwali to drive evil away, and flowers and lights decorate people's homes.

The lunar calendar

Hindu festival dates are based on a lunar calendar, with the 12 months following the phases of the Moon. This means there are only 354 days per year. To match the Western calendar (the Gregorian calendar), an extra month is added every few years. The calendars vary in different parts of India, with months starting at different times in the lunar cycle and with different days for the New Year.

CALENDAR OF HINDU FESTIVALS

Dates of festivals are calculated according to the lunar calendar, based on the movements of the Moon. As a result, dates vary slightly every year if you are looking at the Western, or Gregorian, calendar.

January	Pongal
February and March	Holi Mahashivatri
June and July	Ratha Yatra, Ganesha Chaturthi
August and September	Janmashtami
September and October	Navaratri
October and November	Diwali

Worship and offerings

Hindu worship is called **puja**. It involves prayers (**mantras**) and offering flowers, food and lights to images of Brahman, or a deity, at a Hindu temple (**mandir**) or at shrines set up at home.

In return for offerings, worshippers hope to receive the deity's blessing. Offered foods (called prasad) are eaten afterwards, and are believed to contain the blessing.

Hindu holy books

- The Vedas – include guidance on how to live day-to-day
- The Upanishads – discussion about the relationship of Brahman (the universal soul) and atman (the individual's soul)
- Ramayana – a story about the deities Rama and Sita, and how good overcomes evil
- Mahabharata – an account of an epic war, including the Bhagavad-Gita (epic teachings about how to worship God)

⌃ The Shri Swaminarayan Mandir, Neasden, London, is the biggest Hindu temple outside India.

PONGAL

Pongal is a southern Indian festival that takes place in mid-January. It welcomes the time the Sun is traditionally thought to have reached its southernmost point, and is turning north again. It is a happy harvest festival. Pongal means "boiling". This refers to the boiling of rice and sugarcane in milk to make a dish that is similar to rice pudding. It is offered at shrines and returned, blessed, for eating.

Day 1: Rain deity

The first day of the festival is spent thanking Indra (deity of the clouds and rain, which made the harvests grow). People clean and whitewash their homes to mark a new beginning.

⌃ These women in India are boiling the traditional festival dish for Pongal.

HINDU DEITIES

This list includes some of the main Hindu deities, and the characteristics of Brahman they represent. It also shows some of the festivals they are linked to. In the past, the three main Hindu deities were Brahma (the personal form of Brahman), Shiva and Vishnu. But today, the three main Hindu deities are Mahadevi (great goddess, also called Kali and Durga), Shiva and Krishna (a manifestation of Vishnu). Popular deities include:

Agni – god of fire

Brahma – personal form of Brahman

Durga – mother goddess, family; festival: Navaratri

Ganesha – god of knowledge, remover of obstacles; festival: Ganesha Chaturthi

Indra – god of rain and clouds; festivals: Pongal

Krishna – form taken by Vishnu; festivals: Holi, Janmashtami, Ratha Yatra, Diwali

Lakshmi – goddess of beauty, prosperity; festival: Diwali

Rama – form taken by Vishnu; festivals: Diwali, Dussehra

Saraswati – goddess of knowledge; festival: Saraswati Puja

Shiva – destroyer of the universe; festival: Mahashivratri

Sita – wife of Rama; festivals: Diwali, Dussehra

Surya – god of the Sun, heat and light; festival: Pongal

Vishnu – protector of the universe

⌃ From left to right, these are Brahma, Vishnu and Shiva.

Day 2: Sun deity

On the second day, **kolam** patterns are drawn outside people's front doors to welcome deities in and keep away evil spirits. Pongal rice (see page 8) is cooked and allowed to boil over as a symbol of overflowing thanksgiving to the gods. It is placed on the kolam with flowers, and other foods such as fruit. This is an offering to Surya, the Sun deity, the source of life and heat.

Day 3: Festival of the cattle

On the third day, cattle are washed, their horns are polished, painted and metal caps are put on the ends. The cattle are decorated in flowers, paints, beads and bells. They are allowed to roam freely, and are given boiled rice to eat. The cattle are celebrated in this way because of all the hard work they have done in the fields.

The sacred cow

Cows are sacred to Hindus. As givers of milk, a precious food, Hindus do not harm or kill cows, and do not eat their meat (beef). In India, the killing of cows is against the law. The cow is linked to several deities, including Krishna (who grew up as a cowherd) and also Shiva (who rode a bull).

Kites and bonfires

In western parts of India, Pongal is called Makar Sankranti, and colourful kites are flown. In the northern Indian state of Punjab, the festival is called Lohri. Crowds gather round huge bonfires, which are lit in the harvested fields.

♡ In Punjab and other parts of northern India, Lohri is celebrated on the streets. Fires are lit and dancers perform Bhangra – a mixture of traditional Punjabi and more contemporary dancing.

Case study

PONGAL IN NEWHAM

The **Tamil** community in Newham, England, celebrate Pongal as it is their new year and it marks harvest time. Colourful streetlights brighten the neighbourhood for a week, a street party is held and there are celebrations in the town hall.

Sweet pongal

During the Pongal festival, Hindus cook pongal in an earthenware pot. In this traditional ceremony, they offer the dish to the Sun to thank it for a good harvest.

Please see page 46 for tips on this recipe.

TIME:

About 1 hour

SERVES:

4 people

TOOLS:

weighing scales
large saucepan
stirring spoons
frying pan
small bowl
masher

Vegetarian

Gluten Free

INGREDIENTS:

600 ml water
200 ml milk
120 g white rice
60 g split yellow lentils (moong dal)
30 g butter
40 g chopped cashew nuts
40 g raisins
150 g packed dark brown sugar
50 ml warm water
½ teaspoon cardamom

STEPS:

1 In the large saucepan, heat the 600 ml of water and the milk just until bubbling on medium heat. Add the rice and lentils. Turn down the heat, cover and cook for about 30 to 40 minutes, stirring occasionally to make sure the rice does not stick to the bottom.

2 Meanwhile, in the frying pan, melt the butter on medium heat. Add the cashews and raisins. Sauté (fry) for about 2 minutes. Set aside.

3 In a small bowl, mix the sugar with the 50 ml of warm water. Stir until the sugar dissolves.

4 Mash the rice mixture to break up the lentils and grains. Pour in the sugar mixture. Add the butter mixture and the cardamom. Mix well. Serve warm.

Holi

Holi is a fun-filled and colourful festival. It is a spring festival, celebrated in February or March across most of India and increasingly all around the world. The festival is celebrated in different ways but the liveliest celebration is paint throwing. Different legends are remembered, but the most popular is the story of Prahlad and Holika. "Holi" comes from the name Holika.

⌵ A statue of Holika holding the child Prahlad.

The story of Holika and Prahlad

A demon king ordered his people to worship him instead of God. His son, Prahlad, refused and continued to worship Vishnu. The king tried to kill Prahlad but Prahlad survived being thrown off a cliff, trampled by an elephant and bitten by snakes as Vishnu protected him. The king's daughter, Holika, tricked Prahlad into stepping into a fire with her. She thought she could use her magical powers to stop her burning, but Vishnu pulled Prahlad to safety and Holika burned in the fire. Her powers had vanished because she was using them for evil.

Bonfires

Bonfires are lit for Holi, in memory of the Prahlad and Holika story, and to mark how good overcomes evil. In some parts of India, dummies representing Holika are thrown into the bonfires.

⋁ A bonfire during Holi represents many things, including a celebration of Prahlad's powerful devotion to Vishnu.

Another spring festival – Vasanta Panchami

Another spring festival at this time, celebrated in northern India, is called Vasanta Panchami, which means "yellow fifth" or "spring fifth". Hindus often wear yellow for the festival to welcome spring, and some people fast, too. The fifth refers to the date on Hindu calendars. It is also called Puja, and is a time when Hindus worship Saraswati, the goddess of learning, wisdom, music and the arts (see pages 26–27).

⌃ These villagers are throwing powdered paints near a Krishna temple in western India during Holi. Traditionally, the colours are made from plants.

Paint throwing

One of the most popular traditions at Holi is people throwing coloured powders and water at each other. This happens on the streets and involves the whole family.

Today, all kinds of objects are used to squirt the paint, from plastic bottles to water pistols. However, the story is the same. They throw the paints in memory of Krishna's mischievous nature as a boy, and the pranks he played on the wives and daughters of the cowherds.

Afterwards, everyone goes home and changes into clean white clothes. In the evening, they exchange gifts of food and sweets. The exchange of sweets is part of the spring mood of new starts, forgiveness and peace. Coconut sweets are popular as coconuts are popular offerings at shrines. They are seen as a sacred fruit – pure and good for the health.

Holi events

Some Holi festival events have developed into modern music festivals. Here, crowds are encouraged to throw paint of specific colours all together. These organized events are so popular that they go on tour around the world and even non-Hindus attend the event.

Other popular Holi festival events in the West are more closely linked to Indian cultures and traditions. For example, the Bhangra Dance Company and School draw crowds to their Holi Hai festival at Dag Hammarskjold Plaza in New York City, USA. The event includes traditional Indian music, dance and foods, so it educates a range of New York communities about Indian culture and traditions.

⌃ These traditionally dressed Bhangra dancers are celebrating Holi on the streets of New York.

Coconut
ladoos

TIME:
About 50 minutes

SERVES:
Makes about 24 pieces

TOOLS:
weighing scales
medium frying pan
food processor
spatula
plate

Holi is a colourful holiday filled with fun, laughter and joyful celebration. For example, tossing coconuts into a bonfire is one of the many traditions of the holiday – and we have already seen that coconuts are popular at this festival. These ladoos are fun to make – and eat!

Vegetarian

Gluten Free

INGREDIENTS:

150 g sweetened tender flake coconut
1 teaspoon unsalted butter
¼ teaspoon ground cardamom
250 ml sweetened condensed milk

STEPS:

1 In a food processor, pulse the coconut to chop the pieces finer.

2 Heat the frying pan on the hob on medium heat. Add the butter. When melted, add the cardamom and 100 g of the coconut. (Set aside the remaining coconut on a plate.) Cook for about 1 minute.

Pour in the milk and stir to combine. Stir constantly, scraping the bottom and sides of the frying pan, as the mixture heats up, bubbles and pulls away from the sides of the pan. Cook for about 5 to 7 minutes or until it has formed into a soft dough. Be careful it doesn't start to turn brown and burn.

3

4 Take the frying pan off the heat and let the dough cool for about 20 to 30 minutes. Do not touch it sooner – it will be very hot!

5 Roll a small ball of dough in the palms of your hands. Then roll it, on the plate, in the remaining 50 g of coconut. (If the dough is too sticky, rub your hands with a little butter first.) Repeat with the rest of the dough.

GODS AND BIRTHDAYS

Several Hindu festivals are in honour of the deities. Some Hindus have a favourite deity and three of the most popular are the gods Shiva Krishna and Ganesha.

⌃ These children in Watford painted their faces and are playing music to celebrate the birth of the deity Krishna.

Shiva – the cosmic dancer

Shiva is the destroyer of the universe, often shown in statues as a dancer. On the night of Mahashivratri, marked by a popular festival in February or March, he is believed to do a cosmic dance (called the Tandava). The dance is to destroy the old world so that a new one can be created. The dance rhythms represent the cycle of death and reincarnation.

Hindus fast and worship through the day and night, believing it will free them of their sins and from the cycle of rebirth and death. Indian Hindus have a ritual bath (many go to the river Ganges to do this, as it is regarded as a sacred river). Then they go to the nearest Shiva temple with puja items, such as milk, fruits and oil lamps. Sometimes, long queues of worshippers form at popular temples as they wait to make their offerings.

⌃ Worshippers gather at the Pashupatinath Temple near Kathmandu, Nepal, to make offerings to the god Shiva.

Case study

A Shiva shrine

It is believed that Shiva's home is in the Himalayan mountains. Thousands of **pilgrims** from Nepal, India and South Asian countries gather here for Mahashivratri. They go to the holiest Shiva shrine in the world, the Pashupatinath Temple near Kathmandu in modern Nepal.

⌃ Some 65,000 pilgrims gather every year at the Bhaktivedanta Manor Temple in England to celebrate Krishna's birthday.

Janmashtami – Krishna's birthday

This lively two-day festival takes place around August or September. It is celebrated in different ways all around the world. The biggest celebration in the UK is at Bhaktivedanta Manor, a temple in Hertfordshire. Thousands of pilgrims are given plates of food that has been blessed, called prasad or prasadam.

From cowherd to king

As a child and cowherd, Krishna lived in an ancient forest in Vrindavana, northern India. He had lots of friends, many of them also cowherd boys and girls. When he moved away and became king, his childhood friends missed him so much that they tried to kidnap him and bring him home on a chariot.

Krishna and his chariot

The festival of Ratha Yatra (journey of the chariot) celebrates the story of Krishna's friends attempting to bring him home on a chariot. The biggest festivities are in Puri, north-eastern India. The festival features three chariots containing sacred images of Krishna in the form of a deity called Jagannath, his sister Subhadra and his brother Balarama. Everyone chants the **Hare Krishna mantra** and they also dance.

Chariots

In Puri, the Ratha Yatra chariots are huge, with up to 16 wheels made by hand. Hundreds of people take turns to pull the carts. At the festival in London, the carts are smaller, and for safety only certain people are allowed to push them.

⌃ Like many other major European cities, London has a Ratha Yatra procession every year. This one travelled from Hyde Park Corner to Trafalgar Square.

The elephant-headed god

Ganesha Chaturthi in August or September celebrates the birth of the elephant-headed god, Ganesha. The festival is celebrated all around the world but it is especially popular in western India.

Celebrating Ganesha

Before Ganesha Chaturthi, large numbers of clay statues of Ganesha are made for people to buy. The statues range in size from less than 2 cm (1 in) to over 20 m (70 ft). Special foods are made or bought, and then offered at Ganesha temple shrines and at home. Sweets are popular because legend says that Ganesha liked to eat them.

Ganesha

Ganesha is known for his strength and his ability to move obstacles. **Devotees** pay their respects to Ganesha before puja, or before they set off on a journey or begin any other important activity. They believe he will remove any obstacles from the very beginning.

≫ In places like Mumbai, Hindus honour Ganesha through his statue, which they parade round the streets while singing and dancing.

⋀ After the procession, the Ganesha statues are traditionally immersed or left in rivers or the sea. These Hindus are in Southend-on-Sea in England.

Celebrations around the world

Ganesha Chaturthi is a huge event in many Indian cities, bringing in money for local businesses as hundreds of people buy statues. The event also occurs across the UK, often beside a river, such as the Thames in London or the Mersey in Liverpool.

Now & Then

Keeping waters clean

Many Hindu festivals end with putting statues in water. Worries about polluting rivers or the sea have made people start to put their statues in a bucket or tub of water at home instead.

Saraswati Puja

Saraswati Puja is the celebration and worship of Saraswati, the goddess of learning, wisdom, music and the arts. In some parts of India, this is part of the spring festival, Vasanta Panchami, which takes place in January and February; in others it is part of the Navaratri Festival (celebrated from September to October). Some Hindus celebrate Vasanta Panchami as the birthday of Saraswati.

Learning letters

On the ninth day of Navaratri, musical instruments and books are placed near an image of Saraswati to be blessed. It is seen as a good time for the children to begin to learn to read and write, so young children are taken to the Hindu temples, and in front of an image of Saraswati they are introduced to the alphabet for the first time.

Saraswati (on the top right of the picture) is usually shown with four hands holding symbolic items. These include a mala or string of crystals (representing meditation and spirituality), a book or scroll (knowledge and education) and a musical instrument called a veena (arts and sciences).

Hindu students and school pupils, such as this one in Dhaka, Bangladesh, pray during Saraswati Puja, hoping they will do well in their exams.

Student prayers

Vasanta Panchami and the tenth day of Navaratri are believed to be especially good times to repeat a Saraswati mantra. This is said to lead to a better intellect and memory.

Mother Goddess festivals

Some festivals focus on the Hindu mother goddess, who is known mainly as Parvati (wife of Shiva), a kindly deity. She is also celebrated in other forms, such as the fearsome Durga, who fights evil.

⌃This dance, the dandiya raas, is being performed in Indore, India.

Navaratri – nine nights

Navaratri, which means "nine nights", is an important festival around September and October. It celebrates the mother goddess. It is sometimes called Durga Puja. It focuses on honouring the motherhood, and recalls the legend in which Shiva gave Durga permission to visit her mother for nine days in the year.

Hindus often fast to purify themselves from sins, while others gather for celebratory feasts, music and dancing. Folk dances, such as a fast dance in which sticks are tapped together (called dandiya raas), are popular. Special images of Durga recalling her victory over a buffalo-headed demon, called Mahisha, are worshipped daily.

Dussehra – the tenth day

Dussehra falls on the day after Navaratri. On this day:

- Statues and models of the goddess are put under water, for example in the sacred Ganges river in India, or in the bay at Cardiff in Wales.
- Images made of clay for the festival are returned to clay by submersion in local rivers and ponds or the sea.
- In India, there are performances of a play that tells another important Hindu legend, about Prince Rama and his wife, Sita (see page 31).

∨ A statue of the goddess Durga is carefully immersed in the Thames, London, on Dussehra.

Diwali

Diwali is one of the happiest and most popular of festivals, and it takes place in October or November. It is a time for exchanging gifts, cards and sweets, and for fireworks and lights to be lit. The word "Diwali" comes from a Hindu word that means "rows of lights". Diwali is often called the festival of lights.

Case study

Diwali in Leicester, England

Around 35,000 people attend the switching on of colourful street lights in the centre of Leicester's Asian community. Fireworks, a laser display, music and live entertainment mark the beginning of the festival. For some Hindus who live there, Diwali is also the start of the new year.

Hindus celebrate Diwali for different reasons. In some parts of India, it marks the New Year on the calendar. During Diwali, some Hindus also worship Lakshmi, goddess of wealth and good fortune, and remember the story of Rama and Sita.

Rama and Sita

Prince Rama was heir to the throne, but his stepmother wanted her own son to be heir, so Rama was **exiled** to a forest with his wife, Sita, and brother. When Sita was carried off by the evil demon king, Ravana, Rama asked Hanuman, a monkey general, for help. Hanuman led an army of monkeys into battle and rescued Sita. Rama later killed Ravana with a golden arrow. Rama and Sita returned home so that Rama could become king at last.

"Rows of lights"

Hindus decorate their homes and mandirs with special diva lamps – to welcome Lakshmi and into their houses and temples, which also recalls how thousands of people lit lamps to welcome the **exiled** Rama and Sita home. The lights are also a symbol of the triumph of good over evil.

Five days of Diwali

The celebrations last five days and many Hindus focus on different deities and traditions on each day, including:

- First day: At sunset many Hindus bathe and light a single diva lamp as an offering to Yama, the deity of death.
- Second day: Hindus reflect on a legend in which Krishna defeated a demon called Narakasur. In the evening, fireworks are often set off to ward off evil.
- Third day: Lakshmi is worshipped and women draw rangoli patterns that include tiny footprints of the deity outside their houses. The patterns and footprints are to welcome her blessings of wealth and prosperity into the home.
- Fourth day: On some Hindu calendars, this day is known as Gudi Padwa, a new year's day. It focuses on the love between husband and wife, and gifts are exchanged. It is also celebrated as Annakoot (which means "mountain of food") by some Hindus. Mountains of sweets are offered to deities and 56 or 108 types of food are cooked as an offering to Krishna.
- Fifth day: This day, known as Bhai Duj, marks the strengthening of the bond between siblings. Sisters visit their brothers and pray for their wellbeing. "Bhai" means "brother".

>> Hindu families gather to light a single diva lamp on the first day of Diwali, in temples all around the world.

⌃ Food is prepared and shared in the Shree Swaminarayan Temple in Cardiff just before the Diwali celebrations begin.

A new accounting year

Many Hindu business people complete their yearly accounts during Diwali and offer them to Lakshmi, goddess of wealth and fortune for blessings. They see it as an auspicious (hopeful) time to start the new accounting year. They worship Ganesha as the deity of the removal of obstacles, hoping the new accounting year will have no problems for their businesses.

Vegetarian
curry

Diwali is the festival of lights. This dish is a bright way to celebrate. Serve this vegetable curry with bread or rice. You can adjust the amount of chilli in the dish, depending on how spicy you like your food.

Please see page 46 for tips on this recipe.

TIME:

About 40 minutes

SERVES:

4 people

TOOLS:

weighing scales
knife and cutting board
vegetable peeler
medium saucepan
strainer
large saucepan
stirring spoon

Vegetarian

Gluten Free

INGREDIENTS:

2 potatoes, peeled and diced into small chunks
100 g butter
1 small onion, finely chopped
1 tablespoon finely chopped garlic
1 tablespoon grated fresh ginger
1 teaspoon salt
⅛ teaspoon black pepper

Spices:
 2 teaspoons cumin
 2 teaspoons paprika
 1 teaspoon coriander
 ½ teaspoon cinnamon
 ½ teaspoon cayenne pepper
 1 teaspoon mild curry powder

200 g chopped fresh cauliflower
120 g frozen peas
1 diced green chilli, seeds removed
800 g of tinned chopped tomatoes
150 g plain yoghurt
½ teaspoon sugar

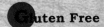

STEPS:

Place the potatoes in the medium saucepan, and add enough water to cover them. Bring to a boil, cover, reduce heat and cook for about 10 minutes until the potatoes are soft. Drain and set aside.

1

2

In the large saucepan, on medium-high heat, melt the butter. Add the onions and cook for about 3 minutes. Then add the garlic and ginger. Cook for another minute. Add the salt, pepper and spices. Cook for about 1 minute more.

Add the cooked potatoes, cauliflower, peas and chilli. Stir to coat. Then add the chopped tomatoes, yoghurt and sugar.

3

4

Mix everything up. Bring just to a boil, and then reduce the heat to medium low. Simmer, uncovered, for about 20 minutes, stirring often, until the cauliflower has softened and the sauce has thickened.

KUMBH MELA

Kumbh Mela is a mass pilgrimage. It is thought to be the biggest religious gathering in the world.

Different ceremonies take place depending on the year. But once every 12 years, Kumbh Mela happens at four sacred river locations in India: the Ganges, Shipra, Godacari and at a point where the Ganges, Jamuna and Sarasvati meet (see map on page 5). The Sarasvati is a mythical river, having dried up long ago. The event is the most spiritually beneficial time for Hindus to bathe in these sacred places.

(see map on page 5)

The elixir of eternal life

The importance of bathing at specific times and places along these rivers is based on a legend. The legend tells of battles between gods and demons over a pot of the **elixir** of eternal life. During the battles, a few drops of the elixir fell in the places where the rivers are now believed to have powers. "Kumbh" means "pot" and "Kumbh Mela" means "festival of the pot".

BELIEFS

Who goes?

The vast crowds who go include:

- **ascetics** (people who live a strict life, denying themselves material comforts, for religious reasons)
- **sadhus** (holy men) who wear robes or are naked and smeared in ash (which symbolizes death and rebirth).

≫ Sadhus wear saffron-coloured robes and cover their faces in grey ash.

Among the activities, there are religious discussions, worshipful singing and people giving out food to the holy men and women, and the poor.

Case study

MAHA KUMBH MELA

Every 12 years, the Kumbh Mela is called Maha Kumbh Mela, and bathing is seen as even more important. In 2013, the main day of the event involved an estimated 30 million pilgrims bathing where the Ganges and Jamuna rivers meet. The festival is so popular it spreads over 55 days, allowing a total of around 100 million pilgrims to bathe.

FAMILY CELEBRATIONS

There are many Hindu customs that mark important stages in a Hindu's life and celebrate family relationships. The traditions vary depending on where, for example, the family lives in India and the **caste** to which they belong. The traditions range from a ceremony on learning the alphabet to the first shaving of a beard.

Jatakarma

One of the first ceremonies a newborn baby experiences is Jatakarma ("jata" means "being brought into existence"). The baby's father uses a gold spoon to put ghee (melted butter) and honey onto the baby's tongue. Ghee, honey and gold are meant to stimulate the baby's intelligence. Mantras for a long life are said near the ear and stomach.

As well as honey, the baby is given a secret name, which is whispered into the baby's ear. It is kept a secret so that enemies cannot use the name in magic spells to harm the child.

Raksha Bandhan

Raksha Bandhan, or Rakhi, is a celebration of the bond between brothers and sisters. The word "Raksha" means protection and "Bandhan" means "to tie".

At the ceremony, the sister says a prayer asking God to look after her brother. She places a red powder mark on his forehead as a sign of being blessed. Then she ties a special bracelet (rakhi) round his wrist. He promises to look after his sister, and gives her a gift. Those without brothers and sisters can also take part in this event because in Hindu families, cousins and close family friends count as siblings.

⌃ Rakhi are made from twisted thread or ribbons, pom-poms, beads and other decorations.

> Flower garlands symbolize the unification of people's hearts.

Weddings

A Hindu wedding marks the beginning of what is believed to be a very important stage of life: the setting up of a new family unit. Marriage is viewed as a lifelong responsibility and the duties involved are explained in the ceremony.

Customs

Hindu wedding customs vary from region to region in India, and around the world. These are some of the main ones:

- A lucky date based on **astrology** is worked out for the wedding.

- The bridegroom is taken to the bride's home or the home where the wedding is to take place, and the bride's parents greet him at the door.

- The couple exchange **garlands** and have a sweet milky drink in front of a specially prepared altar.

- A sacred fire is lit. Offerings, for example roasted grains such as barley, are thrown into the fire, and a priest recites mantras. The couple walk round the fire four times hand in hand. The bride leads the way for the first three circuits, and the bridegroom leads the way for the fourth.

- The couple take seven steps, saying a prayer with each step. This symbolizes their unity, and then their vows are exchanged.

∨ The sacred fire is lit by the priest who also
recites the mantras during the wedding.

Agni

A fire is important in a Hindu wedding as it
symbolizes the fire deity, Agni. The bride and
groom say their promises in front of
the fire because Agni is the main witness of
the wedding. The couple also ask Agni to be
the messenger of their prayers to various
deities.

CELEBRATIONS AROUND THE WORLD

Hindu festivals are celebrated all around the world, often following the same customs but with slight differences. The differences depend on the traditions of the region in India or the country's culture. Highlights of many Hindu festivals involve:

- worshipping deities at home or in the temples
- making offerings
- eating special foods
- street processions
- gatherings on the banks of sacred rivers.

≪ Bhangra dancers performing for the Lohri festival in Punjab, India.

≫ Devotees in Nepal wait to enter the Pashupatinath Temple near Kathmandu for the Mahashivratri festival. Over 80 per cent of people in Nepal describe themselves as Hindus.

◀ Students in Bangladesh celebrate Saraswati Puja.

⌄ Pongal celebrations in Singapore. There are around 160,000 Hindus in Singapore.

◀ Diwali celebrations at the Bhaktivedanta Manor in Aldenham, Hertfordshire, England.

FIND OUT MORE

Books
Hinduism (Special Times), Seeta Lakhani, Jay Lakhani and Jane A C West (A & C Black, 2010)
Hinduism and other Eastern Religions (World Faiths), Trevor Barnes (Kingfisher, 2013)
Hindu Stories (Storyteller), Anita Ganeri (Tulip Books, 2013)
India (Countries around the World), Ali Brownlie Bojang (Heinemann Library, 2012)

Websites
www.bbc.co.uk/food/occasions
Find more celebration foods to cook and taste, such as for Diwali. This website tells you when the festivals are coming up.

www.bbc.co.uk/schools/religion/hinduism
The BBC Schools website has a section covering Hinduism, including information about significant gods and festivals.

www.drikpanchang.com/calendars
Use this website to find the dates of Hindu celebrations on the Gregorian calendar.

www.hindukidsworld.org/index.php/en
Go on this website to find out more about the deities and their stories.

resources.woodlands-junior.kent.sch.uk/homework/religion/hinduism.htm
This website provides some excellent background information on Hinduism, in a factsheet style.

Places to visit
British Museum
Great Russell Street
London WC1B 3DG
www.britishmuseum.org
Explore Indian and Hindu art and objects at the British Museum.

St Mungo Museum
2 Castle Street
Glasgow G4 0RH
www.glasgowlife.org.uk/museums/st-mungos/Pages/default.aspx
St Mungo Museum includes art from all the world's major religions.

You could also contact your local Hindu temple to arrange a visit, for example:
*   Shri Swaminarayan Mandir, London (londonmandir.baps.org)
*   Shree Hindu Temple, Leicester (www.shreehindutemple.net/contact-us/school-visits)
*   Edinburgh Mandir and Cultural Centre (www.edinburghhindumandir.org.uk)
*   Skanda Vale in Llanpumsaint, Carmarthenshire, Wales (www.skandavale.org)

It is a good idea to contact them in advance to arrange to visit. You should always be quiet and respectful in any place of worship.

Further research
As well as the mandirs, which would provide information and help, you could also contact one of the cultural and information centres across the country. For example, the Hindu Cultural Association (Wales) and India Centre, through their website (www.indiacentre.co.uk) or the Hindu Council in the UK (www.hinducounciluk.org).

Cookery tips

Dried spices can lose their smell and flavour if kept too long. The best place to store them is in an airtight container in a kitchen cupboard. Spices stay freshest in dry, cool places out of sunlight.

When you are cooking on the hob, always keep a close watch and stir your ingredients often so they do not burn. Turn down the heat if needed, and always double check that you turn off the rings completely when you are finished.

Vegetable curry and sweet pongal

Sautéing cooks vegetables over high heat with a little bit of fat (such as vegetable oil). It browns the vegetables and brings out their flavours before you add other ingredients.

Vegetable curry

You can buy tinned diced green chilli peppers. If you use fresh ones, be careful. Chilli peppers can irritate your skin and eyes. Cut open the chilli lengthwise (see picture, right). Then remove the seeds and veins with a knife. After this, rinse and dice the chilli into small pieces. When you are done, wash your hands thoroughly with warm soapy water.

GLOSSARY

ascetic person who devotes his or her life to religious beliefs and lives in a disciplined way, with only the basic needs of life

astrology drawing and using charts of the Sun, planets and stars to forecast future events

caste social group in Hindu society; traditionally, Hindu society is split into many castes

deity aspect of Brahman, the One; deities are sometimes called gods

devotee strong believer

dharma power that keeps the world and society going; each person's dharma is linked to their behaviour and values

elixir special liquid; the elixir of life is said to make people live forever

exile be sent away from home, and not allowed to come back

fast go without food or drink for a particular period of time

founder person who first organized a set of beliefs into a religion

garland cluster of flowers and plants

Hare Krishna mantra repeated prayer to Krishna

Indus Valley civilization ancient civilization that was located in what is now Pakistan and northwest India

karma means "action" and relates to how good actions lead to good reactions and bad actions lead to bad reactions. For example, good behaviour leads to a better life when reincarnated.

kolam traditional form of painting, often using rice flour

mandir Hindu place of worship

mantras sacred verses from ancient holy books that are repeated by worshippers

pilgrim someone who travels to visit a particular place for religious reasons

puja worship of or prayer to the deities, including making offerings

sacred very holy and valued highly by religious people

sadhu holy person who dedicates their life to escaping from the cycle of death and reincarnation, traditionally through meditation

shrine place that is sacred because of a link to a particular holy person or object

Tamil people who live in South India and Sri Lanka who speak the Tamil language

INDEX

accounting year 33
Agni 9, 41
Anaankoot 32
ascetics 36
astrology 40
atman 5, 7

bathing, ritual 21, 36, 37
beliefs 5
Bhagavad-Gita 7
Bhai Duj 32
Bhangra dancing 17
bonfires 11, 15
Brahma 9
Brahman 4, 7, 9
brothers and sisters 32, 39

caste 38
chariots 22, 23

dancing 17, 21, 28
deities (gods) 5, 6, 7, 8, 9, 10, 15,
    20–29, 32, 33, 41, 42
demons 28, 31, 32, 36
dharma 5
diva lamps 31, 32
Diwali 6, 30–35
Durga 9, 28
Dussehra 29

family celebrations 38–41
fasting 6, 15, 21, 28
festival calendar 6
festivals 6, 8–35, 42
fireworks 6, 30, 32
food offerings 7, 22, 24, 32

Ganesha 5, 6, 9, 20, 24, 33
Ganesha Chaturthi 6, 24–25
Ganges river 21, 29, 36, 37
garlands 40
Gregorian calendar 6
Gudi Padwa 32

Hare Krishna mantra 22

harvest festivals 8
Hinduism 4–7
Holi 6, 14–19
holy books 7

Indra 8, 9
Indus Valley civilization 5

Jagannath 22, 23
Janmashtami 22
Jatakarma 38

karma 5
kites 11
kolam patterns 10
Krishna 9, 10, 16, 20, 22, 32
Kumbh Mela 4, 36–37

Lakshmi 9, 31, 32, 33
lights 6, 30, 31, 32
lunar calendar 6

Mahabharata 7
Mahadevi 9
Mahashivratri 21
mandirs see temples
mantras 7, 22, 27, 38, 40
music festivals 17

naming ceremonies 38
Navaratri 26, 27, 28–29
New Year 30, 31, 32
newborn babies 38

One, the 5

paint throwing 14, 16, 17
Parvati 28
pilgrimages 4, 21, 22, 36–37
Pongal 8–13
Prahlad and Holika, story of 14, 15
prasad 7, 22
puja 7, 21

rakhi 39

Raksha Bandhan 7, 39
Rama 7, 9, 29
Rama and Sita, story of 29, 31
Ramayana 7
rangoli patterns 32
Ratha Yatra 22–23
recipes
    coconut ladoos 18–19
    pongal 12–13, 46
    vegetarian curry 34–35, 46
reincarnation 5, 21
rice, Pongal 8, 10, 12–13

sacred cows 10
sacred fires 40, 41
sacred rivers 4, 21, 29, 36, 42
sadhus 36
Sarasvati river 36
Saraswati 9, 15, 26
Saraswati Puja 26–27
Shiva 9, 10, 20, 21, 28
Sita 7, 9, 29, 31
soul 5, 7
spring festivals 14, 15, 26
statues 24, 25, 29
street processions 23, 24, 42
Surya 9, 10
sweets 16, 18–19, 24, 30, 32

Tandava 21
temples 7, 21, 26, 42

UK 7, 11, 20, 22, 23, 25, 29, 30, 33
Upanishads 7
USA 17

Vasanta Panchami 15, 26, 27
Vedas 7
Vishnu 9, 14, 15

weddings 40–41
worldwide Hinduism 4

Yama 32